e   op austin 3rd edition

an encapsulat   e most interesting, inspired and authentic
locally owne   shopping establishments in austin, texas

researched, photographed and written by
kaie wellman
cabazon books : 2010

table of contents

eat

shop

kaie's notes on austin

I began this series back in 2003 in my hometown of Portland, Oregon. Seven years later there are 24 cities and counting. I no longer author all of the books myself (insert sigh of relief), but I do still hold on tightly to authoring a couple of cities based on pure affection. Austin is at the top of this list. I can not get enough of this town or the people that live in it. I've been asked many a time if I could define exactly what it is that makes me love it so. Is it swimming in Barton Springs pool at 9pm on a hot night? Is it creating a food pyramid out of barbeque and snowcones? Is it that special breed of Austin storyteller that has me laughing uproariously at every word? I've never been able to put my finger on it, but if I ever do, I'll bottle it up and sell it and be a bazillionaire.

Since the last edition of this book in 2007, the world has changed. People are no longer eating and shopping with brazen abandon. The era of buying five cars because you have a five car garage has (thankfully) passed. People are now seriously thinking about where they want to spend their hard-earned dollars, and more and more people are choosing to spend them locally. Though Austin lost a number of incredible businesses during the dirge (*Los Manitas*, *Anthony Nak*, *Big Red Sun* and *Gardens* to name a few), some new places have taken the brave leap to fill the gap.

Have a fantastic time exploring Austin, whether you're a visitor or if you're a local. And if you need a break from eating and shopping, here are some ideas for you:

1 > *Float on Lady Bird Lake*: Experiencing the water culture around Austin is key, and one of the best ways to do this is to rent a canoe or a kayak. There are plenty of companies to rent from and here are a couple of suggestions: *www.zilkerboats.com* or *www.rowingdock.com*

2 > *SXSW*: Though it's long away from being the little festival that could, *South By* is still a barrel o' fun that not only includes music and film, but also interactive exhibits. Come for one, come for all. It's guaranteed that something will launch here that the rest of the world will be talking about down the line. *www.sxsw.com*

3 > *Visit an Urban Farm*: Austin has more farms within its city limits (many in East Austin) than any other city of its size in the United States. Though most aren't open to the public, others are like *Boggy Creek Farm* and *Green Gate Farms* are open on limited days or have farm stands.
www.boggycreekfarm.com / *www.greengatefarms.com*

4 > *Live Music*: If you come to this town and you don't go see some type of live music, you are stark raving mad. Just pick up a *Chronicle* and point your finger at something and go.

about eat.shop

• All of the businesses featured in this book are locally owned. In deciding which businesses to feature, that's the number one criteria. We also tend to veer away from chains or business "groups" where there are more than four outlets. Then we look for businesses that strike us as utterly authentic and uniquely conceived, whether they be new or old, chic or funky. And, if you were wondering, businesses don't pay to be featured—that's not our style.

• A note about our maps. They are stylized, meaning they don't show every street. If you'd like a more detailed map, pick up a Streetwise map for Austin or we have an online map with the indicators of the businesses noted > map.eatshopguides.com/aus3. And a little note about exploring a city; the businesses we feature are mainly in neighborhoods within the urban core. Each of these 'hoods (and others that we don't cover) have dozens of great stores and restaurants other than the ones listed in this book.

• This is important: make sure to double check the hours of the business before you go, as many places change their hours seasonally.

• The pictures and descriptions for each business are meant to give you a feel for a place, and are the items that the author were drawn to. Please don't take the business to task if what you see or read is no longer available.

• Small local businesses have always had to work their behinds off to keep their heads above water. During these rough economic times, sadly some won't make it. Does this mean the book is no longer valid? No way! The more you use this book and visit these businesses, the better chance they have to thrive.

• The *eat.shop* clan consists of a small crew of creative types who travel extensively and have dedicated themselves to great eating and interesting shopping around the world. Each of these people writes, photographs and researches his or her own books, and though they sometimes do not live in the city of the book they author, they draw from a vast network of local sources to deepen the well of information used to create the guides.

• Please support the indie bookstores in Austin like *Book People*. To find these bookstores, use this great source: www.indiebound.org/indie-store-finder. *eat.shop* also supports the *3/50 project,* it's a great way to include local in your daily life. (*www.the350project.net*)

• There are three ranges of prices noted for restaurants: $ = cheap, $$ = medium, $$$ = expensive

where to lay your weary head

There are many great places to stay in Austin, but here are a few favorites:

hotel saint cecilia
112 academy drive (south austin)
512.852.2400 / hotelsaintcecilia.com
studios from $295 suites from $490
notes: a secluded estate

hotel san josé
1316 south congress avenue (south austin)
512.852.2350 / sanjosehotel.com
standard double from $160 suites from $335
bar: hotel san josé lounge coffee and light snacks: jo's (next door)
notes: legendarily cool austin hotel

kimber modern
110 the circle (south austin)
512.912.1046 / kimbermodern.com
standard double from $250
notes: a small, modern hotel with the intimacy of a bed and breakfast

four seasons austin
98 san jacinto boulevard (downtown)
512.478.4500 / fourseasons.com/austin
standard double from $350 restaurant: trio
notes: it's elegant, it has a spa and it sits on the banks of lady bird lake

w hotel austin (opening december 2010)
200 lavaca street (downtown)
512.542.3600 / starwoodhotels.com
standard double from $275
notes: the w brings it signature style to austin

home away > this company is based in austin and specializes rentals around the world. here's a couple of primo properties in austin to recommend: *www.homeaway.com > p237097, p274021, p235120*

previous editions bizs

eat

anderson's coffee co.
boggy creek farm
caffe medici
carousel lounge
chez nous
clay pit
daily juice
din ho chinese bbq
dirty martin's place
east side cafe
east side pies
el chile
el chilito
enoteca
flip happy crepes
fonda san miguel
foodheads
frisco shop
hong kong supermarket inc
home slice pizza
hoover's cooking
house park bar-be-que
jade leaves teahouse
jeffrey's
jim-jim's water ice
jo's
juan in a million
koriente
la cocina de consuelo
lamberts
la mexicana bakery
little city
mean-eyed cat
mrs. johnson's bakery
nau's enfield pharmacy

p. terry's
phil's icehouse
(amy's ice cream)
phoenicia bakery & deli
polvos
portabla
progress coffee
quality seafood market
sandy's frozen custard
sasha's gourmet russian market
sno-beach hawaiian shaved ice
sunflower
taco deli
teo
the woodland
tiniest bar in texas
top notch
torchy's tacos
vespaio
victory grill
wiggy's

shop

allens boots
amelia's retro vogue & relics
aviary
betty sport
big bertha's
blackmail
eliza page
end of an ear
finch
hem
martinez brothers taxidermist
milk+honey
quincy's guitars
sabia
roadhouse relics
room service vintage
ruth's pinata land
service
solid gold
terra toys
tesoros
texas custom boots
the lightbulb shop
toy joy
uncommon objects
upstairs downstairs
verbena floral design
whetstone audio
yard dog

antonelli's cheese shop

fresh little cheese boutique

4220 duval street. between 42nd and 43rd
512.531.9610 www.antonellischeese.com
tue - sat 11a - 7p sun noon - 5p

opened in 2010. owners: john and kendall antonelli
$-$$: visa. mc
grocery. first come, first served

hyde park >

There's a scene in the movie *French Kiss* where Meg Ryan's character has a transformative experience with cheese. After years of lactose intolerance-induced terror, a train ride through Provence and a smarmy, yet charming Frenchman breaks down her fromage barriers. If you suffer from a cheese phobia, I suggest a visit to the charming (with absolutely no smarm) *Antonelli's Cheese Shop*. Within minutes the knowledgable staff will have you eating out of their hands and you will find yourself besotted with even the stinkiest of cheeses.

imbibe / devour:
'06 chateau du bloy bergerac
ckc farms midnight chevre
ardrahan farmhouse cheese
veldhuizen texas star cheddar
holland marieka aged gouda
l'epicurien apple cider confit
askinosie chocolates
creminelli fine meats

apna bazaar

indian, pakastani and bangladeshi grocery store
8650 spicewood springs road #133b. at 183 frontage
512.249.0202 www.apnabazaaraustin.com
mon - sat 11a - 9p sun noon - 9p

opened in 2008. owner: jozito george
$-$$: visa. mc
grocery. first come, first served

north austin >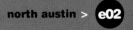

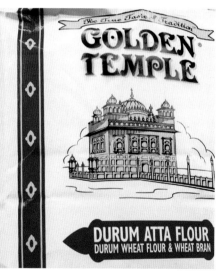

It's a particular quirk of mine, when I'm traveling in foreign lands, that before I head to any monument, temple or museum I aim for the local markets—both the open air markets and the more modern, westernized groceries. I guess then it makes sense here in the States that I'm always sniffing around for great ethnic groceries and *Apna Bazaar* falls firmly into that category with it's mix of Indian, Pakistani and Bangladeshi goods. Even if you don't cook any of these cuisines, this small market is a treasure trove of spices and rices and ingredients that can be used in your everyday diet.

imbibe / devour:
tetley ginger tea
swad almond oil
mdh masalas
golden temple durum atta flour
great selection of spices, beans & rices
reen'as creme glacee exotique
gopi paneer
fresh fruits & veg

arkie's grill

classic austin diner

4827 east cesar chavez street. between springdale and shady lane
512.385.2986 www.arkies.weebly.com
mon - fri 6:30a - 3p

opened in 1948. owners: steve and randy jones
$: visa. mc
breakfast. lunch. first come, first served

east austin > e03

Is there a Church of Fried Chicken? I know there's a Church of Elvis and a Church of the Sub Genius, but certainly somebody has thought that fried chicken is worthy of a place of worship. In Austin I can think of a couple of different spots that sanctify the bird including *Arkie's Grill*. I could go on and on and pontificate up a storm, but all you need to do is take a gander at the hero shot to the left to know this chicken is goooooood. And *Arkie's*, like the great roadside diner that it is, serves up a slew of other comforting vittles which makes this place a Church of Delicious.

imbibe / devour:
texas grapefruit juice
breakfast trash taco
biscuits & gravy
arkie cheeseburger
hensley paramount sandwich
turkey & dumplings
fried chicken
coconut pie

big top candy shop

candyorama
1706 south congress avenue. near annie
512.462.2220
mon - fri 11a - 8p sat 10a - 9p sun 11a - 7p

opened in 2007. owner: brandon hodge
$: all major credit cards accepted
treats. first come, first served

south austin > 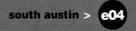 **e04**

Dear parents of children that enter *Big Top Candy Shop*. I implore you—do not walk your kids through this sugar fantasy of a store, allowing them to touch the plethora of candies and gaze at the delights being made at the soda fountain and then tell them, "No treats today honey, maybe next time we visit." Oh the cruelty. I wanted to run after the shell-shocked little girl and shove a couple of Zotz in her back pocket. Instead I stocked myself up on nostalgic goodies, many of which were candy mainstays during my formative years—a Pixie Stix a day keeps the doctor away!

imbibe / devour:
sodas, sundaes & other sundries
hearty italian style meatball bubble gum
toffee crisp
rainbow coconut bar
old faithful peanut cluster
dude, sweet chocolate fungus amongus
salt water taffy
chocolate covered pears & blueberries

casey's new orleans snowballs

icy cold goodness
808 east 51st street. corner of airport
open daily from noon (apr - sep)

opened in 1997. owners: cliff and pattye chapman
$: cash only
treats. first come, first served

north austin > 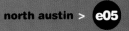

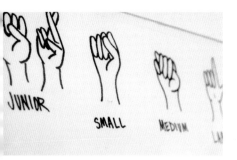

JUNIOR   SMALL   MEDIUM   LA[

Sno-cones. Shaved ice. Water ice. Snowballs. I could explain the differences between these icy delights, but that's a waste of time because they are all #1: cold, #2: sweet, and #3: delicious. If you're going to spend any time in this town during the warmer months, of which there are many, you're going to develop a meaningful relationship with at least one of these cooling treats. My latest fave is *Caseys New Orleans Snowballs*. They make a chocolate snowball (created with homemade chocolate sauce) that will rock your 95 degree world. Though the stand is a bit out of the way, don't let that stop you from a visit.

SNOWBALLS
36 FAT-FREE FLAVORS

imbibe / devour:
snowcones:
  famous chocolate
  leche canela
  dreamsicle
  orchid cream vanilla
  banana fudgesicle
  hurricane
  pink grapefruit

chen's noodle house

divine handcut noodles

8650 spicewood springs road. at 183 frontage
512.336.8888
mon, wed - sun 11a - 9p

opened in 2008. owner: zhao chen
$: cash only
lunch. dinner. first come, first served

north austin > 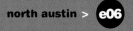 **e06**

Something about this town makes me want to explore its every nook and cranny, including the plethora of ethnic eateries that populate the Northern outskirts. *Chen's Noodle House,* in the same strip mall as *Apna Bazaar* and *Sambet's Cajun Deli*, is a gem that deserves a bit of a road trip. Where do I begin my love letter? This is a stamp-sized spot with all of four tables and a succinct menu of eight items. What inspires rhapsody are the soups brimming with Zhao's hand-cut noodles which in their imperfection are pretty damn perfect.

imbibe / devour:
hot tea
leek pie
green onion pancakes
lamb noodle soup
noodle with egg & tomato
combination soup
lamb skewer
steamed dumplings

chosun galbi

korean barbeque and more
713 east huntland drive. near i35 frontage
512.419.1400 www.chosungalbiaustin.com
open daily from 10a - 10p

opened in 2008
$$: all major credit cards accepted
breakfast. lunch. dinner. reservations accepted

north austin >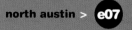

Chosun Galbi is a continuation of the story I began telling at *Chen's*. At the tail end of a day spent circling the outskirts of Austin, I was exhausted from eating, so I figured I would revive myself by eating more at *Chosun Galbi*. There was some solid reasoning behind this as Korean cuisine is known for its restorative qualities. Maybe it's the omnipresent red pepper in Korean cooking, but as soon as I dove into a bowl of spicy crab meat soup, I found new reserves of energy. Or at least enough oomph to get myself to the car and aim towards a cushy sofa with my name on it.

imbibe / devour:
hite beer
bok bunja soju
dwe ji bulgogi (spicy marinated pork bbq)
gam ja tang (pork back bone stew)
kkot gae tang (spicy crab meat soup)
goon mahn doo (dumplings)
bibimbob
gabi soon du bu combo (bbq ribs & soft tofu)

counter cafe

a modern diner

626 north lamar boulevard. corner of seventh
512.708.8800 www.countercafe.com
daily 8a - 4p

opened in 2007. owner: debbie davis
$-$$: all major credit cards accepted
breakfast. lunch. first come, first served

downtown >

I like breakfast well enough, though there are certain things that appeal to me on a menu, that aren't that great when going down the old gullet. I find that steak and eggs fall into this category. I like steak. I like eggs. But when I get tempted to eat them together for breakfast it falls into the category of way. too. damn. much. food. But *Counter Cafe's* quail and eggs is just right and so darn Texan. I think the perfectly grilled split quail and a couple of perfectly fried eggs is a great. way. to. start. your. day.

imbibe / devour:
counter michelada
bellinis
breakfast tacos
counter benedict
texas quail & eggs
the famous pimiento cheese sandwich
polenta fried oysters
counter burger

dai due

roving butcher shop and supper club

austin farmer's market - republic square park. at fourth and guadalupe

512.524.0688 www.daidueaustin.net

sat 9a - 1p

opened in 2006. owners: jesse griffiths and tamara mayfield

$-$$: visa. mc

dinner. butcher shop. classes. first come, first served

downtown > **e09**

Unless you are a hardcore vegan / vegetarian or you're living under a rock, I'm sure you are aware that a trend of meat, meat and more meat has been sweeping the country for a while now. Within this new found love for pork belly and trotters are folks who are embracing the artisinal craft of meat curing and butchering. The couple behind *Dai Due* are a great example. Austinites flock to their farmer's market stand not for meat products, but also their inspired condiments. And if this isn't enough *Dai Due* for you, then book a seat at one of their beloved supper clubs and embrace the deliciousness.

imbibe / devour:
fresh bloody mary mix
wild boar & pepper sausage
bockwurst
boudin blanc
rabbit & olive oil rillettes
jujube paste
southern style pickles
fireman's 4 mustard

dart bowl steak house

bowling and enchiladas, what could be better?

5700 grover avenue. between houston and west koenig lane
512.452.2518 www.dartbowl.com
sun - thu 9a - midnight fri - sat 9a - 1:30a

opened in 1970
$: visa. mc
breakfast. lunch. dinner. full bar. first come, first served

north austin > **e10**

I love bowling alleys. The more old school and slightly frayed the better. Though this is not the original location of *Dart Bowl*, it has been around since the '70s, which is exactly the vibe here. And lest you question whether a bowling alley falls into the category or either eating or shopping, I give you the elegantly named *Dart Bowl Steak house* and in the shop section of this book the *Dart Bowl Pro Shop*. I know many a person who comes here first and foremost for their famous enchiladas and they'll bowl a game or two for good measure. For dessert I suggest M & M's.

imbibe / devour:
chopped steak & two eggs
south of the border migas supreme
cowboy omelette
the famous enchiladas
triple decker club sandwich
mexican patty melt
chicken fried steak
m & m's from the vending machine

east end wines

a great bottle shop

1209 rosewood avenue. corner of 11th
512.904.9056 www.eastendwinesatx.com
mon - wed 10a - 7p thu - sat 10a - 8p

opened in 2010. owner: matt miller
$-$$: all major credit cards accepted
first come, first served

east austin > **e11**

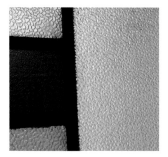

Everybody has secret wishes. I wish I had longer legs, thicker hair and that I had a more refined palate when it came to wine. For example, I would love to be able to define the difference between a Pinor Noir and a Gamay, or be able to connect a wine to it's producer just by the way it tastes. I think my only hope is have the knowledgeable *East End Wines* staff help me out. Mike and crew obviously know their stuff and even when helping out a wine challenged person like myself, they make the complex world world of vino much easier to navigate. Cheers to them!

imbibe / devour:
'08 becker vineyards prairie rotie
'08 block nine pinot noir caiden's vineyard
'08 castillo de monseran garnacha
'08 shinas estate the innocent viognier
'07 laurenz und sophie singing gruner veltliner
unibroue la fin du monde beer
tru organic gin
dripping springs vodka

east side king at the liberty bar

asian-inspired drinking sustenance

1618 east sixth street. between comal and chalmers
512.422.5884 www.eastsidekingaustin.com
daily 7p - 1:45a

opened in 2009. owner / chef: paul qui
$: cash only
dinner. late night. first come, first served

east austin > **e12**

I guess this is as good a place as any in the book to talk in depth about food trailers in Austin. This history of this culture began... oh blah blah blah. There's a zillion different spots you can read about the whole food cart thing and everybody is falling over themselves to explain it. But instead of reading about it, just start experiencing it, i.e., get thee out to eat. And *East Side King* is a good starting spot. Get lubed first at *Liberty Bar* which is the "host" building in front, and then order a round of Paul's Asian-inspired, vegetarian friendly fare. Doesn't this sound like a good way to end your day?

imbibe / devour:
bruxelles biere
curry bun
fried brussels sprout salad
beet home fries
thai chicken karaage
ginger garlic jasmine rice
pro qui's buns
philip speer's homemade cookies

east side showroom

sally bowles would dine here

1100 east sixth street. corner of medina
512.467.4280 www.eastsideshowroom.com
daily 5p - 2a kitchen closes sun - wed 11p thu - sat midnight

opened in 2009. owners: mickie and trudy spencer. chef: sonya cote
$$: all major credit cards accepted
dinner. full bar. late night. reservations accepted for parties of six or more

east austin > **e13**

When you walk into *East Side Showroom* and your eyes adjust from the bright Texas sun to the darkness of the room, you half expect to see a line up of saucily attired, red-lipped, raven-haired, bordello girls attending to languidly lounging customers. Micki has created a bawdy world here that's not only a hoot to hang out in, but one that makes you wish you weren't wearing jeans and flip flops. As you dig into Sonya's delicious locally-sourced fare with cleverly composed drink in hand, forgive yourself for your modern grubbiness and embrace the romance of the *East Side Showroom.*

imbibe / devour:
rum daisy
the diablo
the showroom
antelope tartare
gulf shrimp & curried grits
quail & preserved oranges
lamb ribs with fried okra
crème brûlée

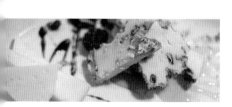

el caribe

salsalicious interior mexican restaurant
5610 north lamar boulevard. near koenig lane
512.452.6207
mon - thu 11a - 9p fri 11a - 910p sat 10a - 10p sun 10a - 9p

opened in 1985
$-$$: visa. mc
breakfast. lunch. dinner. first come, first served

north austin > **e14**

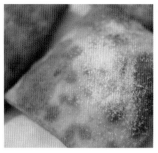

Because a portion of my life is dedicated to a quest for good queso, there's always a place in this book where I must focus on my beloved hot fromage melange. *El Caribe* has good queso. In fact if I wouldn't have had to share with my co-horts and judges of good queso, Joe and Marianne, I would have hoovered the entire bowl here like a glutinous melted-cheese loving pig. I resisted the urge and instead focused on the visually uninspiring, but tastefully inspired, salsa bar. *El Caribe* might be a hole-in-the-wall, but the food is really darn good.

imbibe / devour:
house margarita
strawberry licuados
queso caribeño
tortilla soup
steak à la mexicana
huachinango al mojo de ajo
mojarra frita
sopapillas

el meson taqueria

a little out of the way, but oh so worth it
5808 burleson road. between montopolis and judson
2038 south lamar boulevard. near oltorf
512.416.0749
mon - fri 6:30a - 2:30p sat 7a - 2p

opened in 2001. owners: the macias family
$: cash only
breakfast. lunch. first come, first served

south east austin >

Some people go on vision quests, I go on meal quests. *El Meson Taqueria* is a perfect example of my willingness to go on a trek for deliciousness as it's pretty much between nowhere and nowhere. But despite its location, *El Meson* is definitely a *somewhere* because it's so darn good. The menu is small, the tortillas are a revelation of freshness, and the flavors are perfection. If you aren't willing to go to great lengths like I am though, the kind *El Meson* folks have just opened another location closer in on the South side.

imbibe / devour:
pineapple barrilitos
chorimigas
huevos motulenos
egg & cactus breakfast taco
tinga
calabacitas
enchiladas
chilorio

el naranjo

traditional mexican cuisine served out of a truck

85 rainey street. near red river
512.474.2776 www.elnaranjo-restaurant.com
mon - wed 5 - 10p thu - sat 5p - midnight

opened in 2010. owner / chef: iliana de la vega. owner: ernesto torrealba
$-$$: visa. mc
lunch. dinner. first come, first served

downtown >  **e16**

I'm not sure this is something I want to admit publicly, but I'm all about telling the truth, so here it goes—I don't really like mole. There, it's out. I feel so much better. But now that I've fessed up, *El Naranjo* comes along and confuses me because not only do I like Iliana's moles, I think I might love them. She features a number of traditional Oaxacan moles as specials ranging from a verde to *manchamanteles* (which translates to "tablecloth stainer") which is made from dried chiles, charred tomatoes and ripe fruit. Just the description makes me drool.

imbibe / devour:
sangria señorial
hibiscus iced tea
veracruzanos molotes
empanadas de hongos
cochinita pibil tostadas
chileajo tacos
de garnachas
hongos al ajillo

farmhouse delivery

delivering the farm to your door

512.529.8569 www.farmhousedelivery.com
weekly or bi-weekly deliveries

opened in 2009. owners: elizabeth winslow and stephanie scherzer
$$: visa. mc
grocery on wheels. first come, first served

no storefront > **e17**

I'm a bit embarassed to admit that I have never partici-pated in a CSA. But before you send out the lynch mob, hear me out. I have a small family, we are no Kaie Plus 8, and I we would struggle to eat a weekly ration of a dozen heads of cabbage. This is why *Farmhouse Delivery* is so brilliant. You sign up for their "farm membership," choose weekly or biweekly home deliveries which gets you a reasonably sized mix of produce that is grown at *Rain Lily Farm* (and elsewhere) *plus* you can add meats, cheeses and other food products from carefully vetted local purveyors to your order. Sign me up!

imbibe / devour:
farmhouse blend coffee
zhi tea monk's blend black tea
paqui buttermilk tortillas
pickled dilly beans
rain lily farms herbs, produce & eggs
thunderheart ground bison
love puppies "peanut butter nutcase" brownie
the recipes that come with farm membership

franklin barbeque

trailer barbeque

3421 north i35. corner of concordia
512.653.1187 www.franklinbarbeque.com
wed - sun 11a - sold out

opened in 2009. owner / chef: aaron franklin
$-$$: all major credit cards accepted
lunch. first come, first served

north austin > **e18**

There are not alot of things I would stand in line in searing heat for. But for a good plate of barbeque, I would take the sunburn and armpit outpour. Which is exactly what I did to eat lunch at *Franklin Barbeque*. They open at 11am, but the line forms about 10 minutes before. And you'd best get here before noon because this meaty goodness sells out fast. Grab your order, a cold Big Red, and sit down at one of picnic tables and feel the eyes of the hungry line dwellers upon you. You could gloat as you're devouring the melt-in-your-mouth brisket. But don't, because soon enough you'll be back in that line.

imbibe / devour:
cold big red
sweet leaf tea
pulled pork sandwich
tipsy texan sandwich
two meat plate
any of the meats by the pound
potato salad & pickles
slaw

good pop

new school paletas

1003 barton springs. in the vinny's italian cafe parking lot
512.539.0182 www.goodpops.com
apr - oct tue - sun noon - 8p

opened in 2008. owners: manuel and laura flores and daniel goetz
$: cash only
treats. first come, first served

south austin > **e19**

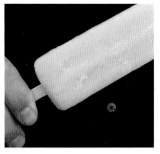

As a kid, nothing was better on a hot summer day than a popsicle. Though ice cream offered a more gentle cooling, the first lick of a popsicle was a cold blast of flavors not found in nature. Cherry popsicles tasted nothing like a real cherry, but more like frozen Kool-Aid. The flavors of the popsicles at *Good Pop*, which have taken their inspiration from *paletas*, actually taste like real fruit because they are made from real fruit, which makes them all natural and all delicious. To note: at press time we learned *Good Pop* might be changing their name and location next year, so check the website to see!

imbibe / devour:
paleta's flavors:
  abuelo's chocolate
  hibiscus mint
  pineapple basil
  watermelon agave
  el cucuy
  banana chile
  tamarindo chile

gourdough's

big. fat. donuts.
1219 south lamar boulevard. across from lamar square drive
www.gourdoughs.com
see website for hours

opened in 2009. owners: ryan palmer and paula samford
$: cash only
treats. first come, first served

Some things that weigh as much as one of *Gourdough's* donuts: a newborn baby, a bowling ball or 120 Hostess mini-donuts. I might be exaggerating a touch, but these suckas are huge. Am I complaining? Hell no! It's just more donut to love, and you can buy one to feed your whole family. Again, just joking, because it's not too taxing to down one on your own. Don't think that you are going to have one for breakfast though, as the rest of your day might be spent in repose. Knowing this, the trailer opens at 5pm, just in time for desert after eating at *Odd Duck* next door.

imbibe / devour:
dublin dr. pepper
donuts:
  mother clucker
  flying pig
  miss shortcake
  naughty & nice
  blue balls
  the puddin'

g'raj mahal cafe

fresh, organic indian

91 red river. entrance on davis
512.480.2255 www.grajmahalcafe.com
tue - thu 5p - midnight fri - sat 5p - 3a

opened in 2009. owner / chefs: sidney and anthony fernandes
$$: visa. mc
dinner. byob. reservations accepted

downtown > **e21**

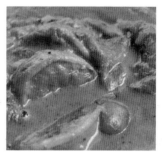

Just to prove to you how mindless I can be while in the midst of the production of these books, it didn't occur to me, until visiting here a couple of times that the way to pronounce *G'Raj Mahal* is Garage Mahal. Word play. Right. Got it. Now that I've got the pronunciation right, I can talk about how I think this is one of the great spots in Austin to spend a warm night. Bring a bunch of friends, some crisp white wine or cold Tiger beer and order this delicious Indian food family style. Then settle in for an incredibly pleasant night amongst the backdrop of the sculptural, skeletal bikes of the *Austin Bike Zoo*.

imbibe / *devour:*
rose lassi
chai
curried lamb samosa
papri chat
shrimp tikka masala
baingan bartha
lamb tikka
indian beignets

hotel san josé lounge

my favorite place for a drink in austin. still.

1316 south congress. between james and gibson
512.444.7322 www.sanjosehotel.com
mon - thu 5p - midnight fri - sun 3p - midnight

opened in 2000
$-$$: all major credit cards accepted
beer / wine. snacks. first come, first served

south austin > **e22**

I feel like I'm having a long-term affair with the *Hotel San José Lounge*. I want to come here looking foxy because this place is so remarkably good-looking. And then once I'm here and am feeling the intensity of the attraction, I morph into full lust looking at the simple, yet desirable, drink and snack menu. Will the sexy, fruit-ridden sangria make me weak at the knees or will the champassion tempt me to throw myself into the pool, à la Anita Eckberg in *La Dolce Vita*? Whatever the draw is, I know that I will keep on coming back again and again and again.

imbibe / devour:
shandy
real ale rio blanco pale ale
tinto de verano
champassion
wine sangria
house marinated olives
tamari roasted almonds
the gorgeous cheeseplate

hut's hamburgers

a classic austin hamburger joint

807 west sixth street. between wood and west
512.472.0693 www.hutsfrankandangies.com
mon - sat 11a - 10p

opened in 1939. owners: mike and kim hutchinson
$-$$: all major credit cards accepted
lunch. dinner. first come, first served

downtown > 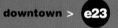 **e23**

This is the third edition of this book and while working on each of the previous books I would find myself driving by *Hut's Hamburgers* thinking about the first time I came here in the early '80s. Somehow with each book, though, I would get seduced by some other classic Austin burger joint and *Hut's* would get the shaft. This time I couldn't ignore it. I swear their neon sign would blink as I drove by, "put me in your damn book!" And so I did. I think it's a requirement to eat at least one burger when you visit Austin, so make sure to head to *Hut's*.

imbibe / devour:
vanilla coke
pink lemonade
the theta special
the sink burger
chicken fried steak
peppered onion rings
fried pickle chips basket
mini corn dog basket

justine's brasserie

a bit o' france in east austin

4710 east fifth street. near spencer lane
512.385.2900 www.justines1937.com
mon, wed - sun 6p - 2a

opened in 2009. owners: justine gilcrease and pierre pelegrin
$$-$$$: all major credit cards accepted
dinner. reservations recommended

east austin >

A restaurant without buzz is like a dog without a bark. Yes there's the serene appeal that comes with silence, but after a while you want some sound. Suffice to say *Justine's Brasserie* is not the basenji of the Austin eating scene, but more like a French bulldog. It's got tons of energy in somewhat of a compact package and it's cute in a toughy type of way. People flow in here from all over town and the energy that comes with the mix is intoxicating. Or maybe the intoxication comes from the drinks that the bar is pouring. Whatever it is, *Justine's* has got the buzz.

imbibe / devour:
l'enfant terrible
muscat de frontignan
escargots a la bourguignonne
aspèrges blanches with sabayon sauce
steak tartare
confit de canard
coquille st. jacques grillé
tarte d'eva

la boîte cafe

the perfect place to start your day

1700 south lamar. corner of evergreen
512.377.6198 www.laboitecafe.com
mon - fri 7:30a - 4:30p sat - sun 8a - 4p

opened in 2009. owners: victoria davies and dan bereczki
$: visa. mc
coffee / tea. treats. light meals. first come, first served

south austin > **e25**

Ahhhhhh *La Boîte*, I have such a crush on you. There are certain places that radiate good vibes and this shipping container/coffee spot/café has it in spades. Maybe it's the way it sits perched on a small hill fronting a strip mall, or the sails that stretch out as awnings. These are nice touches, but really it's the good coffee, delish pastries (some from the best baker in Austin, Barrie Cullinan) and light savories that look good, taste good and are just downright good. It all comes together to make *La Boîte* a place that deserves your affection.

imbibe / devour:
espresso
french press coffee
iced coffee toddy
almond croissant
pain au chocolat
sausage brioche
macarons
ham, gruyere & mustard sandwich

57

la condesa

vivacious, mexico city-inspired cuisine

400 west second street. corner of guadalupe
512.499.0300 www.lacondesaaustin.com
mon - wed 5 - 10p thu - fri 5 - 11p sat 11a - 11p sun 11a - 10p

opened in 2009. owner: jesse herman. chef: rene ortiz
$$: all major credit cards accepted
dinner. full bar. brunch. reservations accepted

downtown >

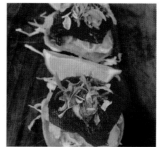

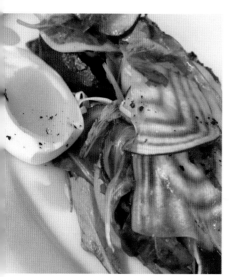

Something about imaginary cities appeals to me more than the real thing. The Paris and New York of my dreams are filled with alluring little side streets dotted with boutiques and bistros that I will sadly never find in real life. I also have an imaginary Mexico City which is boisterous, colorful and filled with mind numbingly good food. This description could also fit *La Condesa* which is inspired by the incredible food culture of MC, from its street fare to its cantinas. The scene here has a spark to it, the décor is vibrant and the food is as pretty to look at as it is delicious to eat. And the best part is that *La Condesa* is real.

imbibe / devour:
el cubico
over 80 varieties of tequila
hamachi ceviche
atun tostada
calabaza
pollo dominguero
costillos de puerco
spicy boca negra

little deli

a classic east coast pizzeria and much more

7101- a woodrow avenue. between piedmont and st. johns
512.467.7402 www.littledeliandpizza.com
mon - sat 11a - 9p

opened in 1992. owner: tony villani
$-$$: visa. mc
lunch. dinner. first come, first served

north austin > **e27**

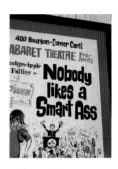

As a native West Coaster who lived in NYC for a number of years, I found myself confused by the description of the pizza at *Little Deli* as "Jersey Shore style." Not so pretty images of Snooki and The Situation filled my head, but then I tasted the pizza and all I could think of was how darn good it was. Still befuddled by the difference between New Jersey and New York pizzas, I asked Tony to explain. He noted that both styles belong under the banner of East Coast style which is derived from Neopolitan, thin-crust pizza. A-ha! Mystery solved. Now I can focus on eating. I'll take a sub to go with my pizza please.

imbibe / devour:
orange crush
new jersey style pizza:
  pepperoni
  rollatini
  white
italian wedge sub
meatball sub
italian cream cake

lulu b's

simple, fresh vietnamese

2101 south lamar boulevard. near oltorf
512.921.4828 www.myspace.com/lulubssandwiches
tue - fri 11a - 4p sat 11a - 5

opened in 2008. owners: laura bayer and christina gustavson
$: cash only
lunch. first come, first served

south austin > e28

Recently, the cult of *banh mi*, the classic Vietnamese sandwich, has moved into the mainstream. I'm loving that I can find these mouth-watering sandwiches more handily now, but I'm bothered by some of the places that are using foodstuffs like peanut butter or American cheese as ingredients. Hello! Really? If you want a modernized version of this sandwich, but don't want the culinary lunacy, head to *Lulu B's* truck. Here they are building *banh mi* that very much mimic the classics, but are lighter and fresher. The same light touch is applied to the other Vietnamese fare here too, and that spells y-u-m.

imbibe / *devour:*
vietnamese coffee
chrysanthemum tea
green bubble tea
banh mi:
  lemongrass chicken
  chinese bbq pork
vermicelli bowls
salad rolls

musashino sushi dokoro

tokyo style sushi

3407 greystone drive (under chinatown restaurant)
at southbound mo-pac expwy access
512.795.8593 www.musashinosushi.com
see website for hours

opened in 1995. owner / chef: takehiko "smokey" fuse
$$-$$$: all major credit cards accepted
lunch. dinner. reservations accepted for parties of seven or more

west austin >

Though I know some people find joy in eating a cream cheese b.l.t. sushi roll, I'm not one of them. I guess I'm a bit of a food purist at heart. When it comes to Japanese fare I like to search out places that feature Japanese food, not Westernized Japanese food. *Musashino* is exactly what I'm talking about. Smokey, the owner/chef, is legendary in town not only for his food, but also for his incredible knife skills. I suggest sitting at the sushi bar so you can watch the food prep choreography behind the counter. It's mesmerizing and the results are delectable.

imbibe / devour:
choya plum wine
takashimizu house sake
sawagani (deep fried mini crabs)
avocado kama
shokado bento
omakase
traditional rolls & american rolls
tempura ice cream

odd duck farm to trailer

where fine dining and food cart culture converge

1219 south lamar boulevard. across from lamas square drive
512.695.6922 www.oddduckfarmtotrailer.com
tue - sat 5:30 - 10p

opened in 2009. owner / chef: bryce gilmore
$-$$: cash only
dinner. first come, first served

south austin > **e30**

There's the saying, "so and so is a bit of an odd duck" and there's cold duck which is cheap bubbly. Then there's *Odd Duck Farm to Trailer* which is neither strange nor liquid, but a fabulous eating experience. Bryce has mixed fine dining with food cartism and come up with a tasty formula. This may well be the only place where a dish like grilled rabbit loin and goat ricotta is served in a paper boat more accustomed to holding greasy nachos. Sitting at the tables here on a warm night with music playing and kids munching their monster *Gourdough* donuts seems like Austin in a lovely nutshell.

imbibe / devour:
ciabatta toast with beets, arugula & goat feta
brussel sprouts with capers & mortadella
soft boiled duck egg, grilled asparagus,
  goat ricotta & toast
ben's salumi with sweet onion & kale salad
1/2 quail with farm potatoes & aioli
grits with cheddar, pork shoulder & farm egg
pork belly slider with carrot & onion slaw

olivia

fine dining with panache

2043 south lamar boulevard. near oltorf
512.804.2700 www.olivia-austin.com
see website for hours

opened in 2008. owner / chef: james holmes
$$-$$$: all major credit cards accepted
lunch. dinner. brunch. full bar. reservations recommended

south austin > **e31**

When people planning to visit Austin ask me about the restaurant scene here, their questions usually focus on barbeque, food carts and barbeque. Very rarely do they inquire about the fine dining options, which is a mistake because they'd miss out on a gem like *Olivia*. This is the type of f.d. establishment that I heart: a pretty room that's inviting and stylish, a wait staff that's knowledgeable and highly professional (too often missing in modern restaurants) and last, but most important, James' beautifully crafted menu tastes dee-vine. *Olivia* gives fine dining a good name.

imbibe / devour:
porta rocha white port cocktail
seductively described wine list
chef's tasting menu
grilled escargot skewer & garlic parsley butter
crispy sweetbreads, radish & maple glaze
seared scallops, trumpet royale mushrooms
local kobe sirloin & frites
duck egg creme brulee

owl tree roasting

local roaster with a big heart
retail: 500 san marcos street (progress coffee). corner of fifth
512.680.7687 www.owltreeroasting.com / www.progresscoffee.com
mon - fri 6:30 - 7p sat 7:30 - 7p sun 7:30 - 5p

opened in 2009. owners: progress roasting llc
$: all major credit cards accepted
coffee. first come, first served

east austin > **e32**

It's hard for me to grasp how certain things work. For example, how is it when I talk into a tiny little box, somebody answers their tiny little box and they can hear my voice? And how is it that by roasting a bitter little bean, something as delicious as a cup of hot coffee can be made? Both are mysteries to me, but the multi-talented Joshua and his partners at *Owl Tree Roasting* can at least answer the coffee question. Here they roast small batches of carefully sourced beans to create coffee not only for their own label, but also for businesses around Austin like *Bird's Barbershop*. Now this I understand.

imbibe / devour:
blends:
  progress house
  mexican chiapas
  jo's
  mohawk
  bird's barbershop brew
  wally 10
  beef & pie beefy's after beer espresso

panaderia chuy

enticing mexican bakery and more
8716 research boulevard #290. at ohlen
512.374.9910
mon - sat 6a - 10p sun 7a - 10p

opened in 2009. owner / baker: chuy guevara. owner: imelda guevara
$-$$: visa. mc
bakery. deli. first come, first served

north austin > 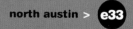 **e33**

Mexican bakeries, *panaderias*, appeal to me. So much so that I find myself going out of my way so I can buy *galleta de grajellas* (oatmeal cookies with sprinkles) or *pan de huevo* (sugared egg bread). Sadly though when I get home and dig into my treasures, they generally never taste as good as they look. Then I found *Panaderia Chuy*. *Madre de Dios*! There's a veritable cornucopia of baked goods here and they all taste as good as they look and Chuy's breads may well be some of the best in town. Going out of my way has never tasted this good.

imbibe / devour:
bolillos
conos rellenos de crema
mantecadas
bombines
besos de fresca
banderillas
ice cream
breakfast tacos & tortas

perla's seafood & oyster bar

a little bit of new england in texas

1400 south congress avenue. corner of gibson
512.291.7300 www.perlasaustin.com
see website for hours

opened in 2009. owner / chefs: larry mcguire and thomas moorman jr.
$$-$$$: all major credit cards accepted
lunch. dinner. brunch. full bar. reservations accepted

south austin >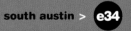

I eat copious amounts of food when I'm working on these books, and most of it (though sadly not all of it) is really good. On occasion one dish will rise above all others to become dish I will dream about until I'm 100 (though if I keep eating this way I won't make it that long). For this book the title goes to *Perla's* lobster stock, cheddar and green onion grits. If my husband and child would not have been with me, I would have devoured the whole thing and licked the dish until my tongue was raw. Instead I shared and happily ate the rest of the glorious seafood we ordered while enjoying the pretty surroundings.

imbibe / devour:
the parasol
(512) wit beer
half dozen half shell oysters:
  sheepscott (maine)
  totten inlet (washington)
ahi tuna tartare with quail egg
lobster stock, cheddar & green onion grits
steamed wreckfish

rosita's al pastor

al pastor destination

1911 east riverside drive. between parker and royal crest

512.442.8402

restaurant daily 8a - 10 stand mon - tue 9a - 1a wed - sun 9a - 3a

opened in 1985. owner: rosita juarez

$-$$: visa. mc

breakfast. lunch. dinner. late night. first come, first served

south east austin >

Al pastor, for those of you who don't know, is grilled pork that is marinated with chiles and other sometimes secret ingredients and then spit-grilled in the style of Lebanese *shawarma*. It is then used most famously in tacos, but can be found in other traditional dishes as well. In Austin many places advertise themselves as having the "best *al pastor* in town." Since I have not eaten at all of the literally dozens and dozens of places that promise this, all I can say is *Rosita's Al Pastor* serves up some pretty mouth-watering grilled meat. Let that stand as my official endorsement of deliciousness.

imbibe / devour:
coca mex
micheladas
isauras "que'es eso queso"
huevos rancheros
al pastor tacos
torta cubano
carne guisada dinner
tamales by the pound

77

sambet's cajun deli & firey foods store

where to get your cajun on

8650 spicewood springs road #111. at 183 frontage
512.258.6410 www.sambets.com
mon - thu 11a - 8p fri - sat 11a - 9p

opened in 1970. owners: catherine and doug slocumbe
$-$$: visa. mc
lunch. dinner. grocery. first come, first served

north austin >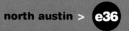

I think this place has the longest name of any of the businesses featured in this book: *Sambet's Cajun Deli & Firey Foods Store*. The time it takes you to say this, is about the same amount of time it would take you to realize that your tastebuds were burning from one of the hot sauces they sell. Even if this place wasn't in my favorite food strip mall in Austin (see *Apna Bazaar* and *Chen's Noodle House*), I'd still go out of my way to eat their savory Cajun delights, and spend an hour trying to figure out which of the zillions of hot sauces to take home with me.

imbibe / devour:
sweet tea
muffaletta
po' boys
crawfish etouffe
deep-fried turkeys
fresh live crawfish
alligator meat
hundreds of hot sauces

smitty's market

legendary barbeque

208 south commerce. between market and prairie lea
512.398.9344 www.smittysmarket.com
mon - fri 7a - 6p sat 7a - 6:30p sun 9a - 3p

opened in 1999. owner: nina schmidt sells, jim sells and john fullilove
$-$$: visa. mc
breakfast. lunch. early dinner. first come, first served

lockart > **e37**

Smitty's Market is not in Austin. In fact, Lockart, the town where *Smitty's* is located, is a fair distance from Austin though it's often noted as being on the outskirts. So even though I usually only feature bizs in the urban core of a city, I couldn't resist the call of *Smitty's* with it's big open fire working barbeque magic on prime pieces of Texas pork and beef. Sitting in the main room here makes you feel like Lockart is frozen in 1968 and though there is a legendary feud that's often spoken about in conjunction to this spot, all I, and you, should care about is how ridiculously good their barbeque is.

imbibe / devour:
by the pound:
  brisket
  sausage
  ribs
beans
cheddar cheese
pickles
white bread

tâm deli & cafe

go-to spot for authentic vietnamese
8222 north lamar #d33. between powell and meadowlark
512.834.6458
mon, wed - sun 10a - 8p

opened in 1999. owners: mrs. tam, mrs. phuc and mrs. minh
$-$$: visa. mc
lunch. dinner. first come, first served

north austin >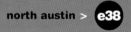

There are Pointer sisters, Andrew sisters and unfortunately Hilton sisters, but none can hold a candle to the sisters behind the delicious Vietnamese food at *Tâm Deli & Cafe*. Though not all of the sisters are involved at *Tâm* on a daily basis, the feeling of family is pervasive and the cooking reflects it. For example the kumquat lemonade is made with the fruit that comes from one of the sisters' kumquat trees. What I wouldn't give to get an invite to one of their family meals. Oh wait, coming here is probably just as good.

imbibe / devour:
fresh kumquat lemonade
jicama spring roll
shrimp & shredded yam crispy fritters
vietnamese crepe
garlic butter shrimp banh mi
rice vermicelli with grilled lemongrass beef
sweet rice with banana & red beans
bahh choux

texas french bread

beloved austin bakery-turned restaurant

2900 rio grande street. corner of 29th
512.499.0544 www.texasfrenchbread.com
dinner tue - sat 6 - 10p (see website for additional hours)

opened in 1987. owners: murph, ben and judy wilcott
$-$$: all major credit cards accepted
breakfast. lunch. dinner. bakery. reservations recommended

midtown >

If you think I'm going to talking about bread here, you'd be wrong. Yes, *Texas French* Bread is a bakery and has long been an Austin institution helmed by Judy Wilcott. But then her sons Murph and Ben decided that it was time to give *TFB* a twist and they began hosting dinners. And when I say dinners, I don't mean something slopped on toast. The Wilcott boys serve beautiful food that has foodies citywide a-twitter (both literally and figuratively). My meal here was delicious, but I will admit I spent a good deal of my evening with my eyes glued to the dessert case. This is a bakery after all.

imbibe / devour:
alice's french toast
house granola & white mountain yogurt
la niçoise on focaccia
pimento cheese on whole wheat sourdough
tagliatelle & seafood puttanesca
black drum with oven roasted beets
pan seared bavette steak with frites & aioli
butterscotch budino

the original hoffbrau

no nonsense steak

613 west sixth street. between rio grande and nueces
512.472.0822 www.originalhoffbrausteaks.com
tue - sat 11a - 2p, 5 - 9p

opened in 1934. owners: mary gail hamby ray and ruben n. ray
$-$$: cash only
lunch. dinner. first come, first served

downtown >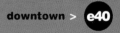

Americans are crazy about their steakhouses and seem perfectly willing to plop down hundreds of dollars for a rib eye or New York strip if it's served in a clubby, low-light atmosphere. So what's a carnivore to do if they don't want to take out a second mortgage to eat a steak? They go to the legendary *Original Hoffbrau*. Here you can get a steak bathed in a melted, buttery substance, salad, potatoes, crackers and a slice o' white bread for a mere pittance. And if you sit inside you can still get that dark room vibe, with maybe a bit (okay alot) less glamorous surroundings.

imbibe / devour:
sweet tea
shiner bock
steaks:
  ribeye
  large t-bone
  new york strip
green salad, potatoes, crackers
onion rings

thom's market

the little market that could

1418 barton springs road. corner of jessie
512.479.9800 www.thomsmarket.com
mon - sat 8a - 10p sun 10a - 8p

opened in 2007. owners: bill and beth thom
$-$$: all major credit cards accepted
grocery. first come, first served

south austin >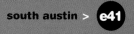

What would happen if you took a *7 Eleven*, refitted it with warm lighting and an orange cooler, featured organic and locally-sourced products and had a staff that occasionally zoomed around on roller skates? You would have *Thom's Market*. Situated in a primo location on the way to Barton Springs, *Thom's* is not only convenient like a quick stop place, but offers all the amenities of a much bigger store. As a topper, it's owned by a family who make you feel like you're walking into a friends house. I'm thinking the only thing that could make *Thom's* better would be to offer roller skating lessons with purchase.

imbibe / devour:
jasperilla old ale
watermelon cream oogavé soda
andersons coffee
wateroak farms goat yogurt
hines jumbo salted peanuts
sifers valomilk
white castle frozen cheeseburgers
useful sundries

uchi / uchiko

modern japanese cuisine

uchi: 801 south lamar boulevard. across from juliet
uchiko: 4200 north lamar boulevard. between 42nd and 43rd
512.775.1224 www.uchiaustin.com
see website for hours

opened in 2003. owner / chef: tyson cole
$$-$$$: all major credit cards accepted
dinner. full bar. reservations recommended

south austin / north austin >

I'm not a big fan of celebrity chefs, nor do I watch The Food Network. So why do I think Tyson Cole, chef and owner of *Uchi*, is the bees knees? He of Iron Chef fame, with features in every form of print media known to man? It's simple—because his food is sublime; gorgeously sourced and prepared and always interesting, making *Uchi* a one-of-a-kind eating experience in Austin. Wait, that is until *Uchiko* came along. Yes, Tyson has taken the *Uchi* show to the North side and though this newly hatched spot wasn't open when I finished this book, I have no doubt it will be just a spectacular as its sibling.

imbibe / devour:
uchi:
  shiro nuta
  omaaru ebi
  chef's tasting menu
uchiko:
  mame yaki
  wagyu momo
  umaso makimono

whip in

a 7/11 this is not

1950 south ih35. corner of mariposa
512.442.5337 www.whipin.com
daily 10a - midnight

opened in 1986. owners: the topiwala family
$-$$: all major credit cards accepted
breakfast. lunch. light dinner. beer / wine. grocery. first come, first served

south austin > **e43**

Not to be confused with the classic Devo ditty, "Whip It," the *Whip In* is a destination in Austin that's become a classic for it's amazing beer and wine selection, Texas meets Gujarat-style snacks and soooo much more. There's something in Austin's DNA that breeds convenience stores with attitude. Sure you could come here and pick up a pack of smokes and six pack of something cold, but you'd be missing out on what makes the *Whip In* so brilliant. I mean, what other fast stop place has live music and an in-house brewery? None I tell you.

imbibe / devour:
vast, eclectic collection of wine & beer
the obama shandy
egg & cheese naan with cilantro chutney
toasted panaani's:
  travis heights
  78704ever
chana masala bowl
mary louise butter brownies

• downtown
2nd street district

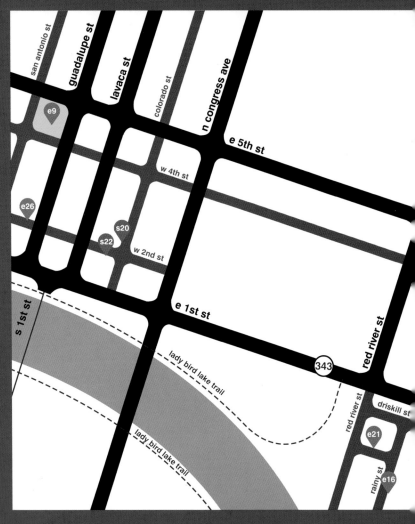

eat

e9 > dai due
e16 > el naranjo
e21 > g'raj mahal cafe
e26 > la condesa

shop

s20 > if+d
s22 > mercury design studio

note: all maps face no

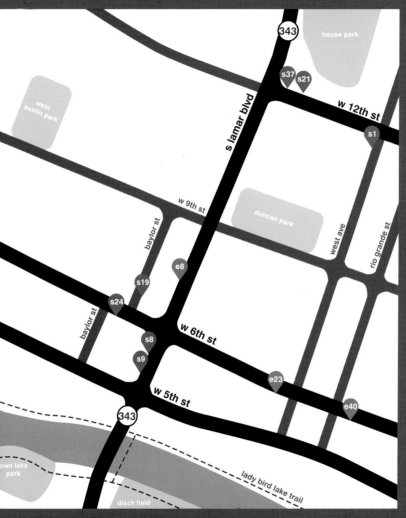

downtown •
clarksville

eat

e8 > counter cafe
e23 > hut's hamburgers
e40 > the original hoffbrau

shop

s1 > 12th street books
s2 > by george men
s9 > by george women
s19 > howl interiors
s21 > kick pleat
s24 > nest modern
s37 > underwear

all maps face north

• east austin

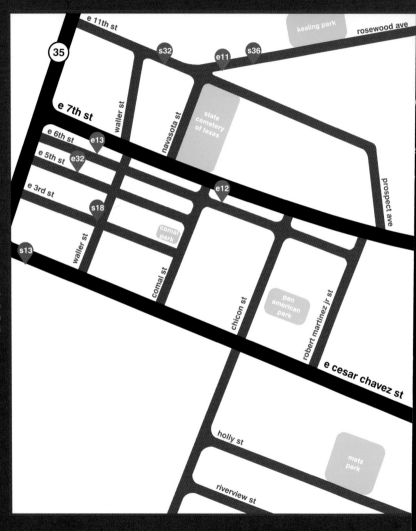

eat

e11 > east side wines
e12 > east side king
e13 > east side showroom
e32 > owl tree roasting

shop

s13 > domy books
s18 > helm
s32 > switched on
s36 > trailer space records

note: all maps face n

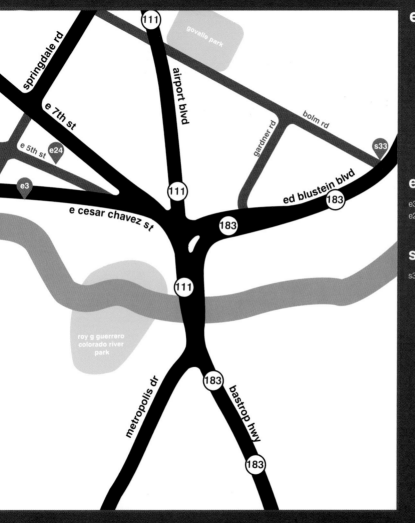

eat

e3 > arkie's grill
e24 > justine's brasserie

shop

s33 > texas state surplus facility

note: all maps face north

• midtown
ut / the drag

eat
e39 > texas french bread

shop
s4 > bell and bird
s10 > catbird paper
s11 > complete clothing
(not on map)
15 > fiddlers green music shop
s25 > nice kicks
s27 > rootin' ridge toymakers

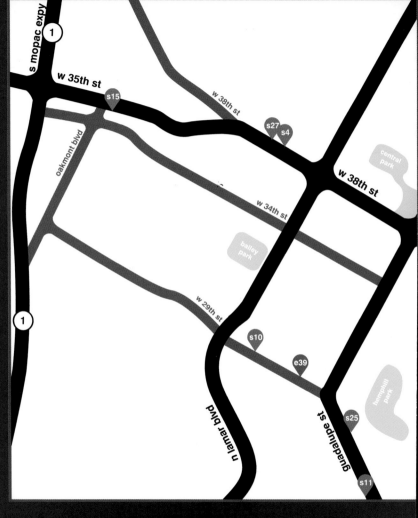

note: all maps face north

midtown •
hyde park

eat

e1 > antonelli's cheese shop
e5 > casey's new orleans
snowballs
e18 > franklin barbeque
(off map)

shop

s5 > blackbird
s7 > breakaway records

note: all maps face north

north austin

eat

e7 > chosun galbi
e10 > dart bowl steak house
e14 > el caribe
e29 > musashino sushi dokoro
(off map)
e27 > little deli

shop

s3 > austin bike farm
s12 > dart bowl pro shop
s23 > mod green pod
s29 > spruce upholestery
s34 > the corner shoppe mall
s38 > uptown modern

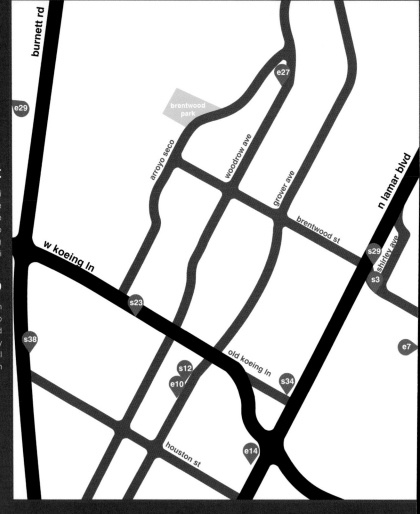

note: all maps face nor

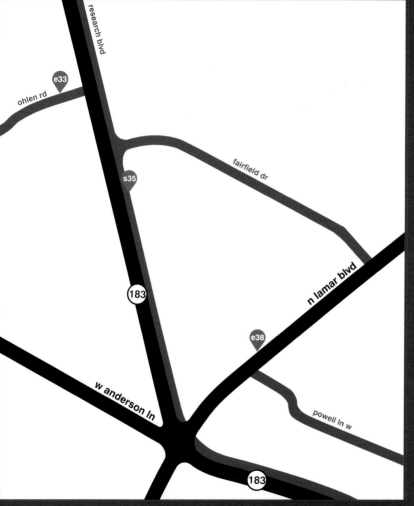

north austin

eat

e33 > panaderia chuy
e38 > tam's deli & cafe

shop

s35 > tiny's western shop

note: all maps face north

eat

e2 > apna bazaar
e6 > chen's noodle house
e36 > sambet's cajun deli &
firey foods store

183

pond springs rd

mcneil dr

spicewood springs rd

e2

e36

e6

parliament rd

jollyville rd

research blvd

183

barrington way

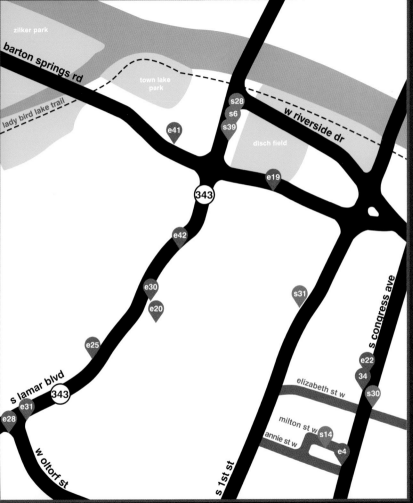

south austin

eat

e4 > big top candy shop
e19 > good pop
e20 > gourdoughs
e22 > hotel san josé lounge
e25 > la boîte
e28 > lulu b's
e30 > odd duck farm to trailer
e31 > olivia
e34 > perla's seafood & oyster
e41 > thom's market
e42 > uchi

shop

s6 > bows + arrows
s14 > feathers
s28 > spartan
s30 > stag
s31 > stitch lab
s39 > w3ll people

note: all maps face north

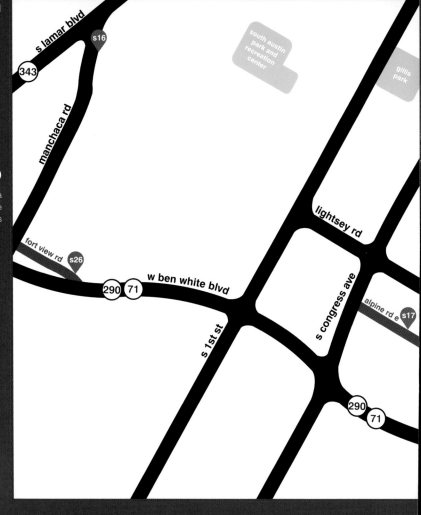

south austin

shop

s16 > ga ga
s17 > habana house
s26 > roadhouse rags

note: all maps face north

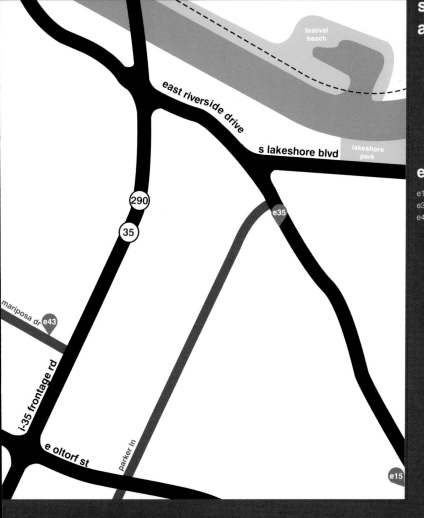

south east austin •

eat

e15 > el meson taqueria
e35 > rosita's al pastor
e43 > whip in

note: all maps face north

12th street books

antiquarian books
827 west 12th street. between shoal creek and west avenue
512.499.8828 www.12thstreetbooks.com
mon - fri by chance or by appointment sat 10a - 6p

opened in 1992. owner: luke bilberry
all major credit cards accepted
online shopping. book appraisals

downtown >  **s01**

The saying, "can't see the forest for the trees" certainly pertains to my overlooking *12th Street Books* for the last two editions of this guide. It's not that I didn't love this antiquarian / vintage bookstore, it's that I never saw it. Over the years I've driven up and down this street zillions of times, but somehow this cloaked gem was hidden from my view. And oh what I was missing—a den- like space full of gently aged treasures of the written word and sumptiously illustrated art books. I could have easily spent all day in here, but now that it's on my radar returning over and over again will be a breeze.

covet:
agee on film by james agee
hornblower and the hotspur by c.s. forester
*memoirs and secret chronicles of the courts
  of europe: marie antoinette*
les diners de gala by salvador dali
marchel duchamp by octavio paz
mastering the art of french cooking
  by julia child, loisette berthold & simone beck

alyson fox / a small collection

beautifully crafted simplicity
www.asmallcollection.com / www.alysonfox.com
by appointment only

opened in 2007. owner: alyson fox
all major credit cards accepted
online shopping. custom orders / designs. commissions

no storefront >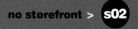

Alyson Fox's name was familiar, but for the life of me I couldn't connect a face to the name or even confirm that I knew Alyson. Instead of trying to figure out the puzzle, I just got on with meeting her and was struck by the multitude of talents she has. Almost everywhere I looked in her studio (and beyond) I saw something she had created. Whether it was a necklace, a photograph or a silk-screened piece of clothing, each was produced in very limited quantities. And then it came to me, I had seen her work at *Candystore Collective* in SF. The two degrees of eat.shop seperation was in full force here.

covet:
limited edition alyson fox designs:
  totes
  raw silk silkscreen tanks
  colored bead necklaces
  brass spider bottle opener
  ink dish collaborative dinnerware
  necklace with wood cube & turquoise bead
  drawings & photography

austin bike farm

new bikes. old bikes
6516 shirley avenue. just off lamar
512.419.1911 / 512.585.0127 (emergencies) www.austinbikefarm.com
tue - sat 11a - 7p

opened in 2010. owners: owen weber and kristy sangster
visa. mc
repairs. custom orders

north austin > **s03**

I can't tell you how many days in a row I drove North on Lamar to see if *Brazos Trading Company* was open, its pile of old Schwinns and well worn Levis tempting me through the dusty window. One day in a fit of frustration after finding it closed again, I drove around the corner and there was a sign for *Austin Bike Farm*. A sign from the bike gods? I followed it and came upon where old bikes not only come to die, but also come back to life when people buy their parts. Add on new bikes for sale, bike repair and a possible cafe in the future—yes, the bike gods are happy.

covet:
new bikes:
  linus
  commençal
  blkmrkt
  183rd street
  civia
vintage bikes
parts & more parts

bell and bird

exquisite custom and antique jewelry

1206 west 38th street #1102. near lamar in the 26 doors plaza
512.407.8206 www.bellandbirdjewelry.com
tue - fri 11a - 5p sat 11a - 3p or by appointment

opened in 2010. owners: rhianna horan and cyrus shennum
all major credit cards accepted
custom design / orders

midtown >  s04

When I'm working on these books, I fantasize that I will discover a place that leaves me speechless. *Bell and Bird* fulfilled this dream. Pause for a moment of silent awe. What has me verklempt about *B & B* are the timeless, sublime pieces of antique jewelry that the lovely couple, Rhianna and Cyrus, have gathered from far and wide. Much of the jewelry here is from the century before the last century, which means when you buy one of these pieces you'll become part of the long storyline and journey that your new found heirloom treasure has been on.

covet:
antique:
  tiara ring
  14k wedding bangle
  aquamarine earrings
  opal diamond topaz ring
  cut steel chandelier earrings
  tiffany robin's egg scent holder necklace
  mourning jewelry

blackbird

stylish clothing and accessories for very little dosh
112 east north loop boulevard. near avenue f
512.904.9114 http://blackbirdaustin.blogspot.com
tue - sat 11a - 7p sun noon - 6p

opened in 2010. owners: stacey breakall and juliana azar
all major credit cards accepted

hyde park >

It would be nice to always have a big wad of dosh to buy beautifully crafted clothing, but sometimes your desires and your pocketbook are at odds. So before you take drastic measures and head to the mall, I suggest going to *Blackbird*. Not only are the clothes here super affordable, the owners Stacey and Juliana tell a enticing retail story with moody hues and Frenchy stripes. And if your boyfriend is feeling a bit light in the wallet, bring him here too because there's a good selection for guys. Being price conscious doesn't mean you have to lose style consciousness.

covet:
esley
yue zhi meng
tov
uno core
down east
johnny max
handmade headbands
ju ju jewelry

bows + arrows

clothing and accessory fundamentals for the modern urban shopper

215 south lamar #c. near riverside
512.579.0310 www.shopbowsplusarrows.com
mon - sat 11a - 7p sun noon - 5p

opened in 2008. owner: lauren wilkins
all major credit cards accepted
online shopping

south austin >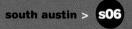

There are a many modern terms that are overused, but the one that grates on me the most is BFF. It's just so Paris and Nicole that I want to scream. It's not that I'm opposed to good friends; take for example the side-by-side businesses *Bows + Arrows* and *Spartan* (see page 161). This is friendship at it's finest. *B + A* is the clothing part of this alliance and Lauren gives as much attention to women's clothing as to men's, focusing on fashion forward lines that are known for their classic simplicity. Based off all the things I want here, I'm thinking Lauren and I might be future BFFs, if I can force myself to say it.

covet:
steven alan
shipley & halmos
karen walker
apc
band of outsiders
manu by lauren manoogian
n.d.c. boots
portland general store

breakaway records

all vinyl, all the time
211 west north loop. at chesterfield
512.538.0174 www.breakawayrecs.com
daily 11a - 8p

opened in 2008. owner: gabe vaughn
all major credit cards accepted
turntable repair

hyde park >  **s07**

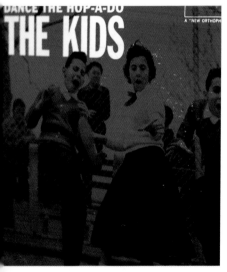

I don't have a turntable because I gave it away along with my Captain & Tennille and Henry Gross records. But now I need a turntable again. I'm tired of the soul-less quality of CDs and MP3s. I want to hear the buzz and scratchiness of a needle skimming along vinyl; I want to hear the yowling of Joey Ramone or Screamin' Jay Hawkins the old school way. And so I'll go to *Breakaway Records* and buy myself a vintage turntable, and while I'm at it I'll stock up on vinyl, both new and old. Then I'll lock myself in a room just like I'm 15 again, and listen to music until my head spins happily.

covet:
vinyl:
  gino washington *out of this world*
  the pure sound of the purifys
  units *new way to move*
  tangerine dream *stratosfear*
  little joe & la familia *brown stuff*
sterling 45 receiver
astrex solid state turntable

by george men

sharp men's fashion

524 north lamar boulevard. between fifth and sixth
512.472.5951 www.bygeorgeaustin.com
mon - sat 10a - 7p sun noon - 6p

opened in 1977. owners: matthew and katy culmo
all major credit cards accepted

downtown >  s08

Since 2008, stories in the media about the state of retail have been nothing but bad news. It got to the point where it was just too depressing to pick up a newspaper. So when *The New York Times* went looking for a positive story in conjunction to retail, it's no surprise they chose *By George*. Matthew and Katy are retailer extraordinaires, and know how to roll with the punches. In the midst of the dirge, they reintroduced men's clothing, which is fantastic because Matthew is a menswear expert. Everything here is not only fashionably sharp, it's also totally wearable. Perfect for Austin.

covet:
levis xx
golden goose
porter bags
post overalls
billy reed
simon miller
maison martin margiela
lanvin

by george women

sharp ladie's fashion
524 north lamar boulevard. between fifth and sixth
512.472.5951 www.bygeorgeaustin.com
mon - sat 10a - 7p sun noon - 6p

opened in 1977. owners: matthew and katy culmo
all major credit cards accepted

downtown >

I think Katy Culmo and I are the middle-aged version of the Olsen twins. We aren't related, but we look a bit alike, are the same not-so-tall height (don't say short, please) and have a similiar style of dressing. When I'm walking around looking at the women's clothing at *By George* with her and she notes pieces she is drawn to, it's on the tip of my tongue to say how much I like the same, whether the piece is drop-dead elegant or casually simple. She understands fashion is not something to be slavish to or make you into a Stepford, it's to have fun with, whatever your budget looks like. That's right sister.

covet:
nili lotan
dosa
hazel brown
gary graham
raquel allegra
zero+ maria cornejo
coclico
current elliot

catbird paper

pretty papers

900 west 29th street. corner of pearl
512.436.8506 www.catbirdpaper.com
mon - sat 10a - 4p

opened in 2008. owner: joy speer
all major credit cards accepted
custom design / orders

midtown > **s10**

During the working day I type, text and twitter and I've noticed over the last couple of years my handwriting has begun to suffer due to my reliance on electronics. My once beautiful, sloping script has become an ugly, jagged scrawl. So the prescription I've given myself is to start writing more notes and letters. The perfect place to find proper accoutrements is *Catbird Paper*. This slightly off the beaten path spot has a perfectly pretty selection of all things paper, including their own line of goods. Goodbye texts, hello letters!

covet:
catbird press invitations, announcements
 & correspondence
elum
hello lucky
snow+graham
cavallini
roost
gianna rose atelier

complete clothing

streetwear joint
1904 guadalupe street. corner of martin luther king jr.
512.473.8244 www.complete-clothing.com
mon - thu noon - 7p fri - sat noon - 8p sun 1 - 5p

opened in 2006. owner: zaul zamora
visa. mc
special orders

midtown >

While working on this book, I got stuck on one of the UT side streets during a massive run-a-thon. As I sat idling away, I noticed how many of the runners were wearing UT emblazoned outfits, which is obviously *de rigeur* if you attend. Friends, I want you to know there's a whole world of clothing out there for you that's not burnt orange and it can be found at *Complete Clothing*, right in your 'hood. Zaul has pulled together a great selection of both clothing and sneakers that will make you look fresh without making you look ghetto. Shopping here shows you're learning something.

covet:
stussy
undefeated
huff sf
primitive
benny gold
clae
the hundreds
g-shock

127

dart bowl pro shop

everybody needs their own bowling bowl, don't they?

5700 grover avenue. between houston and west koenig lane
512.452.2518 www.dartbowl.com
mon noon - 7 tue noon - 5:30p wed - thu noon - 8 fri 3 - 7p sat 11a - 4p

opened in 2003. owner: ron eubanks
all major credit cards accepted
custom design / orders

north austin > s12

Here's the mistake most people make when it comes to bowling—they don't have their own ball. My bowling life changed dramatically when I got my own ball. The holes were drilled to fit my fingers and I chose the perfect weight ball for my mediocre abilities and strength. Don't you see the need to come to the *Dart Bowl Pro Shop*? It's a father/son operation and these two know their stuff. Still on the fence? Listen, balls are not that expensive and second, you can get one with a name like Zephyr that smells like blueberries and is multi-colored. Now are you convinced?

covet:
bowling balls:
  storm "invasion"
  storm "reign of fire"
  maxion "captain midnight"
  hammer "vibe"
  track "spare"
dexter shoes
hilton bowling shirts

domy books

progressive things to read

913 east cesar chavez. corner of san marco
512.476.3669 www.domybookstore.com
mon - sat noon - 8p sun noon - 7p

opened in 2008. owner: dan fergus
all major credit cards accepted
online shopping. gallery

east austin > **s13**

I love books, which you might have guessed because I'm a publisher. But to be more specific, though I love many different genres of books, I have special feelings for art books. I could get all print-geeky on you and talk about how the interaction of ink on paper is infinitely intriguing to me, but I'll focus more on the base level of attraction: art books are beautiful to look at, and *Domy Books* is filled with the most eclectic, titillating collection in Austin. If I went MIA in this town, the first place someone should look for me is here amongst the stacks, happily reading away.

covet:
the complete film works by robert frank
tiny art director by bill zeman
like lipstick traces by numerous authors
obsessive consumption by kate bingaman-burt
shovel in a hole by urs fischer
apocalypse cakes recipe cards
mags & zines
magda sayeg's yarn bombing

feathers

desirable women's vintage clothing

1700b south congress street. enter on milton
512.912.9779 feathersboutiquevintage.blogspot.com
daily 11a - 7p

opened in 2005. owners: masha poloskova and emily hoover
all major credit cards accepted

south austin > **s14**

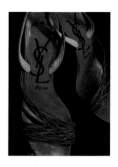

It takes a fair amount of panache to pull off wearing vintage clothing, and what I mean by that is nobody wants to look like Carol Brady sporting a '70s pantsuit or like Donna Summer in one of her less fortunate '80s era disco get-ups. The way to make vintage look modern is to not mimic the past, but to take bits and pieces of it and incorporate it into your style. *Feathers* is the perfect place to get some lady fabulous pieces, whether it's a pair of YSL stilettos or a Bill Gibb's mink halter top. Throw your new purchases on with a skinny pair of jeans and kapow, you're super-stylin'.

covet:
vintage:
  jody california
  shopping with anthony
  gunne sax
  geoffrey beene
shoes:
  halston
  a. gomez

fiddler's green music shop

a strummer's wonderland

1809 west 35th street. between mo-pac and jefferson
512.452.3900 www.fiddlersgreenmusicshop.com
tue - sat 10a - 6p thu 10a - 8p sun noon - 5p

opened in 2008. owners: clay levit and ben hodges
visa. mc
online shopping. classes. lessons. repairs. jams

midtown >

Ever since I heard the riff at the end of Rod Stewart's song *Maggie May*, I have loved the sound of the mandolin. For half my life I have been telling myself I must learn how to play one, though I figure it might be smart to learn how to play a guitar first, which I'm still working on. Walking around *Fiddlers Green Music Shop* lit the mandolin fire inside me again, as this is a mandolin wonderland. Here you can find instruments for beginners or professionals, some hand-crafted, and a whole raft of other stringed instruments. Coming here makes me itch to start a-strumming as well.

covet:
collings mandolins
ellis mandolins
resonator ukeleles
o'hana ukeleles
vega banjos
vintage gibson banjo
dusty strings harps
tim kerr artwork

ga ga

if i were only a little kid again

2810 manchaca road. corner of lamar

512.462.4510

mon - sat 10a - 7p sun noon - 6p

opened in 2010. owner: caroline hernandez

all major credit cards accepted

registries

south austin >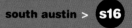

Even though the word gaga has been co-opted by an outré, Saran Wrap-wearing pop star, I still associate the term with the cooing sound of babies. It's what I'm assuming Caroline was thinking when she named her charming new children's store *Ga Ga*. Though I am of the belief that it's a parental right to dress your kids in cute clothing, I get a little scared when adults gussy up their tykes in styles that make them look like they should be at Studio 54. You won't find those get ups here, instead you'll find fun, modern clothes that celebrate childhood.

covet:
decaf plush
axel & hudson
knuckleheads
stella industries
cardboard designs teepee
dwell studio bedding
plan toys drumset
dante beatrix backpacks

137

habana house

home of the ash hall of fame

3601 south congress avenue (behind ruta maya). off of woodward
512.447.9449 www.showmeyourash.com
mon - thu 10a - 9p fri - sat 10a - 10p sun noon - 6

opened in 2004. owner: michael rocha
all major credit cards accepted
online shopping. smoking area

south austin > **s17**

Disclaimer: This blurb does not suggest you start smoking, smoke more or stop smoking. End disclaimer. Now I can let you know that all the world's problems are being solved at *Habana House*, which is a first class cigar shop. A few comfy chairs let regulars sit and discuss world affairs and such with Jim (the manager and moderator) while puffing away on fragrant stogies. The day I was there the guys were tackling the gulf oil spill and pretty much had the problem figured out when I left 30 minutes later. The next time the G7 summit happens, I think they should have it at *Habana House*.

covet:
cigars:
  perdomo "connecticut" toro
  dion "illusione" line
  tatuaje
  don pepin garcia black edition
  romeo y julieta habana reserve
nat shermans
pipe tobacco

GRAN FABRICA DREW ESTATE S.A.

helm

beautifully crafted, handmade men's shoes
1200 east third street #3. near waller
512.609.8150 www.helmhandmade.com
by appointment only

opened in 2009. owner: joshua bingaman
all major credit cards accepted
online ordering. custom orders / design

east austin > s18

Joshua Bingaman is a multi-tasking master. When I first met him he had just opened *Progress Coffee*, which is at the forefront of eco- and socio-concious coffee houses. Then he decided it was time to get into roasting which begat *Owl Tree Roasting* (see page 71). Somewhere in his downtime he began *Helm*, a handmade shoe concern. How does one man do it all? In Joshua's case, he's got a great team behind him which includes the Turkish crafts-men who cobble these new style with an oldfangled twist shoes. A pair will immediately identify you as someone who wears their individuality proudly.

covet:
helm styles:
  brock
  emi
  poppy
  ray ray
  samuel
  tante
  dunkel

howl interiors

furniture and curios for the urban bohemian

603 baylor street. near sixth
512.731.9928 www.howlinteriors.com
by appointment only

opened in 2005. owner: barry jelinski
visa. mc
online shopping. pop up shops

downtown > **s19**

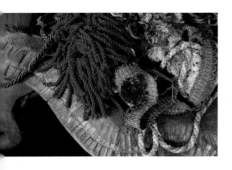

Barry, the mad genius behind *Howl Interiors* had my full attention after uttering just two words: Grotto Revival. Brilliance! I've got nothing against Mid-Century Modern or Shaker, but enough already. I've been searching for that special creative someone who uses the techniques of shock and awe which is certainly Barry's modus operandi. The Grotto style he's riffing off of goes back to 18th century Italy where classical furniture was embellished in a rococo style with natural elements. Barry's modern day approach might take the form of an octopus cocktail table or a winged Jesus. Now I'm shocked and awed.

covet:
coquillage
turkey jesus
neptune cocktail table
leo in a box
coke bottle collage
custom farmhouse tables
hand-carved neptune cocktail table
grotto revival etagere

143

if+d

furniture. gifts. sarcasm.
208 colorado boulevard. corner of second
512.469.0870 www.ifdaustin.com
mon - sat 10a - 6p sun noon - 5p

opened in 2005. owner: kristen bolling
all major credit cards accepted
online shopping. custom orders / design

downtown > **s20**

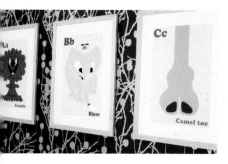

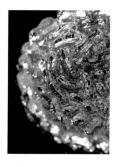

I'm not so hot at figuring out acronyms, but I do get some jollys by taking stabs at them. For example, I'm thinking that *IF+D* stands for I Forgot + Dined or Intestinal Fortitude + Depravity. It could also stand for Interesting Furniture + Design, but I'm thinking Kristen, whose cheeky humour shines through in this furniture and design outpost, wouldn't create such a straight moniker. Whatever it stands for, more importantly you can buy Blu Dot furniture here which is Insanely Fantastic + Dy-no-mite and there are many clever accessories to surround your new furniture with. Instant Fabulosity + Delight!

covet:
blu dot anything
gus modern delano chair
scrap daddy end table
mash studios lax coffee table
jamie borlant human decoy
harry allen peanut bowls
mike merritt "hacked" idea dishware
mark mcginnis alphabet prints

kick pleat

clothing i want to wear

918 west 12th street. near lamar
512.445.4500 www.kickpleat.com
mon - sat 10a - 6p sun 1 - 5p

opened in 2004. owner: wendi koletar
all major credit cards accepted
online shopping

downtown > **s21**

It's been five years now since I wrote the first Austin book, and I have met most of the owners of the businesses that are featured except Wendi, the owner of *Kick Pleat*. I was convinced there was no Wendi, but instead a mysterious person with a great sense of style, constantly rumored to be in Paris or some other exotic locale. She became the Banksy of the Austin retail scene to me. But then someone professing to be Wendi introduced herself to me last week in NYC. This woman certainly looked chic, sporting the signature *Kick Pleat* modern, yet highly wearable wardrobe. Was it Wendi? Who knows.

covet:
hache
rachel comey
a piece apart
sofie d'hoore
humanoid
acne
ld tuttle
soulita bags

mercury design studio

vivid lifestyle and home design store

209 west second street. near colorado
512.236.0100 www.mercurydesignstudio.com
mon - sat 10a - 7p sun 11a - 6p

opened in 2005. owner: steve shuck
all major credit cards accepted
custom orders / design services

downtown > **s22**

Though I'm a happy person, I like the color gray. I love heather gray clothing. I think dove gray walls are chic. My favorite color of car is charcoal gray. Something about this gray fixation makes me worry that I'm secretly dour or soon to be heading that way. To make sure this doesn't happen, I'm heading to *Mercury Design Studio* to get my color fix. Walking in here is energizing. Every corner tells a different color story, each more vibrant than the last. Steve not only mixes tones, he mixes products; reworked vintage furniture to luscious scarves to unusual jewelry. Color me happy.

covet:
reinvintage:
  house line of repurposed furniture
john derian
taschen books
seda france
geode jewelry
niven morgan
jonathon adler

mod green pod

modern organic cotton upholstery fabric
1507 west koenig lane. between woodrow and burnet
512.524.5196 www.modgreenpod.com
by appointment only

opened in 2006. owners: nancy mims and valerie pearcy
visa. mc
online shopping

north austin > **s23**

Even before the now defunct *Domino Magazine* reawakened the wallpaper desire in me, I was dreaming about having walls that went beyond satin, eggshell or gloss as a decorative element. So it's a bit sad that I still don't have a stitch of wallpaper hung. I'm hoping *Mod Green Pod* might be the place that gets me off my behind. These patterns are so compelling, so contemporary, so graphically fresh that it makes me want to wallpaper the whole house, inside and out. And while I'm at it I might cover the cars, the pets and anything else that I can use *MGPs* fabrics on. I feel a transformation coming.

covet:
fabrics:
  bloom
  grand jubilee
  glimmer
wallpapers:
  delight
  butterfly jubilee
tote bags

nest modern

a place to kit out your human nest

1009 west sixth street. corner of baylor
512.637.0600 www.nestmodern.com
mon - sat 10a - 6p sun 1 - 5p

opened in 2005. owners: john allison and douglas galloway
all major credit cards accepted
custom orders / design services

downtown > **s24**

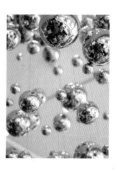

Sometimes when I'm trying my best not to work, I'll watch the birds outside my window make their nest. It's fascinating to see the intensity that goes into gathering all the little twigs and leaves and ground cover to make their shelter cozy. If I had the vigor and attention to detail in accordance to my abode, I would march myself over to *Nest Modern*. There are so many beautiful, useful necessities to choose from to kit out a home. From furniture, to lighting, to the softest rugs my toes have ever dug into, this place makes nesting a pure joy.

covet:
gus modern anything
particle chandelier
pebbles hand-tufted rug
mu a stool
volcanic planters
suavo double walled teapot
studio dr fandango 5 pillow
blomus

nice kicks

sneaker freaker heaven
2815 guadalupe street. between 28th and 29th
512.320.8100 www.nicekicks.com
mon - sat 11a - 8p sun noon - 6p

opened in 2010. owners: matt and allison halfhill
all major credit cards accepted
online shopping

midtown >  **s25**

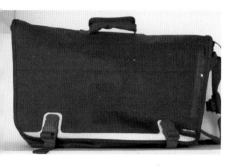

When it comes to footwear, I'm somebody who talks the language of No. 6 clogs or Rachel Comey wedges, meaning I couldn't begin to tell you what's of the moment in conjunction to sneakers. That's why I'm sending you to *Nice Kicks*, because Matt knows everything I don't know and more. Heck he's got so many zillions of people reading his blog, he could put together his own *Nice Kicks* army of sneaker freakers many of whom show up at this über-cool store the moment a limited edition shoe hits the shelves. Watch out though, I might be the first in line.

covet:
shoes:
  nike air max 90 "infrared"
  converse auckland racer
  nike air max 95 "grape"
  the supra avenger
  nike air mariah
  off-white canvas "wino" supra skytop
good wood jesus

roadhouse rags

vintage store, recording studio and performance space
1600 fortview road (ben white westbound access). between banister and manchaca
512.762.8797 www.myspace.com/roadhouserags
daily noon - close

opened in 2006. owners: clay connell and kelli archer
cash only
shows

 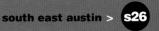

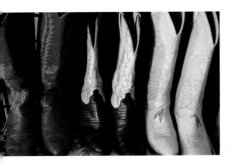

Roadhouse Rags is a retail first for *eat.shop*. It's not only a vintage store, but also a recording studio and concert venue. I'm thinking while they're at it they should add a corn dog vendor and a ping-pong court. Okay, that's taking it a bit far as *Roadhouse* is pretty durn perfect the way it is. What got me here was the not too big, not too small collection of vintage Western wear and ladies '50s party pretties. I was sure when I went out back to the outdoor stage there would be some couples swinging around dolled up in duds from here. There weren't, but I'll be back soon to fill the void.

covet:
vintage:
  western shirts
  cowboy boots
  purses & jewelry
  sleepwear
  purdy ladies party wear
  california pottery
live recordings

rootin' ridge toymakers

hand crafted wooden toys

1206 west 38th street #1105. near lamar in the 26 doors plaza
512.453.2604 www.rootinridge.com
mon - fri 10a - 5p sat 10a - 4p

opened in 1975. owners: georgean and paul kyle
visa. mc
custom orders / design

midtown >  s27

If your three year old asks you to buy her a Squinkies Gumball Surprise and you can't bear another piece of plastic in your house, there's a fantastic alternative: a handcrafted wooden toy from *Rootin' Ridge Toymakers*. Though plastic toys are everywhere we look, chances are they aren't going to be heirlooms, but instead a part of our ever growing landfills. Paul at *Rootin' Ridge* makes toys that your child will play with and love now, but will be something they can give to their children thirty years from now. These are the types of toys that make childhood special.

covet:
rootin' ridge wooden toys:
  push rattle
  timbali
  texas native animals puzzle
  texas aggravation puzzle
  wheeled animals
  mason bee bungalow
  bird feeder

spartan

a bit of wonderul this and a bit of fantastic that

215 south lamar #b. near riverside
512.579.0303 www.spartan-shop.com
mon - sat 10a - 7p noon noon - 5p

opened in 2008. owner: currie person
all major credit cards accepted
online shopping. registries

south austin > **s28**

I'm fully out of the closet as a lazy shopper, which you might find surprising because I shop for a living. But truth be told, I sometimes have a hard time getting myself motivated to get in my car and go out a-searchin' for a present. This is why when I find a place like *Spartan* (the neighbor to *Bows + Arrows*), I go a little cuckoo and want to buy everything in the place. There's such a brilliant array of beautifully designed and original items here that I can fill my gift coffer to the brim with loads of goodness. This way when the gift need arises I just walk back to my closet, which is a lazy shoppers dream.

covet:
clare vivier clutches & bags
the wild unknown great lakes prisms
laura lombardi stacked rectangle necklace
simplemente blanc soaps
fruitwood cheese boards
chester wallace bags
kevin patrick mccarthy lights
erin considine jewelry

spruce

furniture redesign studio

6607 north lamar. corner of brentwood
512.454.8181 www.spruceaustin.com
mon - fri 10a - 6p sat noon - 4p

opened in 2008. owners: amanda brown
all major credit cards accepted
online shopping (etsy). classes. custom orders / design

north austin > **s29**

I want you to know that even though I'm sure I'd like you, you are not welcome to come to my house. I know this sounds rude, but I would be too embarassed to have you see my ratty couch that has been gnawed on by a long succession of stinky dogs. I would invite you to come to my house though if I got my disintegrating couch reupholstered at *Spruce*. Or, even better, I should throw the couch out and get a new couch, chairs and lamps here. Whether it's new upholstery you need or a funky throw pillow or a piece of furniture, the ladies here will have you covered. Sorry for the pun.

covet:
the beatnik barry white sofa
cupid chairs
willie pillows
the care bear chair
cherry clossom chairs
rising tide settee
flames of passion headboard
custom lampshades

stag

heritage brands for men

1423 south congress avenue. corner of elizabeth
512.373.stag www.stagaustin.com
mon - thu 11a - 7p fri - sat 11a - 8p sun 11a - 6p

opened in 2009
owners: ted allen, steve shuck, don weir, joel mozersky and bobby johns
all major credit cards accepted
online shopping

south austin > **s30**

The heritage tag has been applied to many things: heritage roses, heritage turkeys, heritage toys. But the biggest heritage splash might well be within the clothing industry, especially in the men's sector where heritage brands like Levi's, Pendleton and Quoddy are all the rage. An offshoot of this has been the emergence of some extraordinary retail ventures like *Stag*. It's a blast to explore here with the mix of clothing, accessories, taxidermy, found objects and ephemera. This isn't just shopping, it's experiencing —which makes the activity all the more enjoyable.

covet:
ralph lauren rrl
life after denim
oliver spencer
franklin and gower
penfield
beckel canvas
raen eyewear
vintage workboots

stitch lab

where to get your sewing juices flowing
1000 south first street. across from the texas school for the deaf athletic field
512.440.0712 www.stitchlab.biz
mon - sat 11a - 6p sun 1 - 6p

opened in 2009. owner: leslie bonnell
all major credit cards accepted
classes

south austin > **s31**

Though the crafts of yesteryear have made a big comback recently, and I know a slew of knitters and felters, many friends have secretly shared with me that sewing scares them. I understand this, as it petrifies me. Even though I come from a long line of talented sewers that includes my grandmother, mother and daughter. But *Stitch Lab,* surprisingly, didn't scare me. In fact being here made me want to sew. From the moment I walked in and saw the cool fabrics and the cozy rooms set up with sewing machines, I felt the terror of the featherstitch disappear. Maybe I can be crafty after all.

covet:
fabrics:
  alexander henry
  echino
  moda
sublime stitching patterns
vintage figurine pin cushions
vintage deadstock zippers
classes galore

switched on

music electronics store
1111 east 11th street. at waller
512.782.8806 www.switchedonaustin.com
sun - tue noon - 8p wed - sat noon - 9p

opened in 2010. owners: chad allen, john french and guy taylor
all major credit cards accepted
online shopping. repairs

east austin >  **s32**

You've got to imagine that a girl who played in a synth pop band called Matisse Video in the mid '80s is going to have a jones for a vintage synthesizer store, which is why the tractor beam of synth sounds pulled me to *Switched On*. Not only are there primo vintage Moogs and Casios here, there are also brand new thingamajigs like the cool thingomagoop. Though I'm the furthest thing from a tech geek, this place makes me want to spend hours (days even) fiddling about making crazy sounds and wonky beats.

covet:
rhodes mark one stage piano
wurlitzer mlm (music learning machine)
estey m101 travel organ
maestro rythm king
morley wah-wah pedal
roland g77 bass guitar
bleep labs thingomagoops
doepfer maq 16/13 midi sequencer

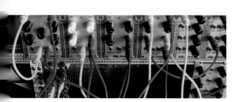

texas state surplus facility

yards and yards office supplies
6506 bolm road. at smith
512.463.1990 http://portal.tfc.state.tx.us/surplus/state
mon - fri 8a - 4:30p

visa. mc.

east austin > **s33**

When it comes to shopping, I like to mix it up a bit. And where better to mix it up then at the *Texas State Surplus Facility*. Coming here is like shopping at a football field filled with rows of used filing cabinets and office desks. Throw in, for good measure, tabulating machines and computers from the early '90s and hundreds of misplaced Swiss Army Knives (does everyone lose these?) and you've got a rough sense of this place. If I'm making the assortment of goods sound a bit rote, think again. There are treasures to be found here and the prices harken back to the '70s. You'd be foolish not to dig around for a spell.

covet:
file cabinets
desks
bookshelves
typewriters
desk chairs
credenzas
hockey sticks
swiss army knives

the corner shoppe mall

a trove o' taxidermy

5900 north lamar boulevard. old koenig lane
512.451.7633 www.taxidermyking.com
mon - sat 9a - 6p

opened in 1986. owner: john brommel
all major credit cards accepted
online shopping. appraisals

north austin > **s34**

Animal lovers please hear me out. I am an animal lover too and I don't relish the idea of shooting and then stuffing Gentle Ben. But I do have a soft spot for taxidermy, especially in the context of visiting Deyrolle, the legendary natural history shop in Paris. Even though *The Corner Shoppe Mall* is on a non-descript corner of Lamar instead of the Left Bank, it has a pretty magnificent collection of taxidermy, some of which might work into the décor of my house. Okay maybe not the hyena, but the squirrel driving a toy car could be a good conversation piece.

covet:
taxidermy:
bears
exotic deer
pheasant
warthog
water buffalo
horns
mexican blankets

tiny's western shop

mexican rodeo and western wear shop

8403 research boulevard. between fairfield and clearfield

512.476.1277

mon - sat 10a - 8:30p sun noon - 6p

opened in 1949. owner: gloria worsham

all major credit cards accepted

custom orders / embroidery

north austin > **s35**

I have never been to a *charreada* (a traditional Mexican rodeo) and last I looked at my busy calendar, I don't have plans to go to one. But won't stop me from going to *Tiny's Western Shop*. It's chuck full of gear that one might wear if they were competing in or going to a rodeo, or if they are like me, just love Western wear. There's a wealth of goodness to be found here from white leather moccasins to little kid's guayberas to customizable pins you can attach to your cowboy hat (or whatever you like). *Tiny's* is pretty mighty in my esteem.

covet:
clothing:
  meztizos
  resisto rodeo gear
  wrangler pro rodeo competition gear
  rocky mountain jeans
dos de oro boots & cowboy hats
minnetonka moccasins
cowboy hat pins

trailer space records

ts loves rock n' roll

1401 -a rosewood avenue. corner of angelina
512.524.1445 www.trailerspacerecords.com
tue - sat noon - 10p sun noon - 6p

opened in 2009. owner: spot
cash only
live music

east austin > 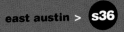 **s36**

When I was in high school and college it didn't occur to me to hang out at a record store. Not sure why, maybe it was because the local pizza place had cuter guys. Maybe if *Trailer Space Records* existed back in my day, I would have hung out here. I'm sure there are not only some cute guys that work here, but more importantly there's great music to be bought and live music to listen to when bands play on the stage that's in the midst of the store. Yeah, I think I can wrap my head around this hanging at the record store thing and you should too.

covet:
lps by:
    bad sports
    the golden boys
    pygmy lush
    the big dirty
    wild america
    nature boys
    mind spiders

underwear

luscious lingerie
916b west 12th street. near lamar
512.478.1515 www.shop-underwear.com
mon - sat 10a - 6p noon 1 - 5p

opened in 2004. owner: elizabeth tigar
all major credit cards accepted
online shopping. registries. special orders

downtown > **s37**

What is it with people wanting to go commando? I just recently spent an otherwise perfectly nice night with friends that was sullied with all the talk of commando-ism. I'm pretty sure if these gals shop at *Underwear,* this piccadillo will go out the window. The underthings here are just so pretty, with everything from super romantic boudoir lingerie to everyday bras and panties. And lest you worry about looking like a Pussycat Doll, Elizabeth buys incredibly fashion forward lines that are both tasteful and sexy. So ladies, put your panties back on and get yourself some *Underwear.*

covet:
mimi holliday
stella mccartney
blush
eberjay
myla
the lake and stars
huit
jimmy jane

uptown modern

great vintage finds

5453 burnet road. near west koenig lane
512.452.1200 www.uptownmodernaustin.com
mon - sat 11a - 6p sun noon - 5p

opened in 2007. owner: jean heath
visa. mc
wish lists

north austin > 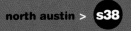 **s38**

My entire adult life I have lived in older houses that often have had a fair amount of hand-me down furnishings. Because of this I have a fantasy of someday building a modern, low-slung house. Something that would use lots of wood, stone, a fair amount of concrete and modern furniture. Even though my vision is modern, I know that to give this fantasy dwelling soul I will mix in vintage furniture and *Uptown Modern* would be the perfect spot to shop. Jean carries a wide selection of mid-century pieces including outdoor pieces and vintage clothing to boot. Fantasy house, here I come.

covet:
'70s tufted leather couch
'50s hans wegner folding chair
'60s gem locke leather chairs
'60s west german floor vase
'60s salterini bench
'70s elephant head necklace
enticing collection of vintage clothing & accessories

w3ll people

eco-conscious beauty products
215 south lamar #b. near riverside
512.366.7963 www.w3llpeople.com
mon - sat 10:30a - 6p sun noon - 5p

opened in 2008. owners: shirley pinkson, dr. renee snyder and james walker
all major credit cards accepted
online shopping

south austin > 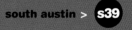 s39

W3ll People makes me want to be a healthy, glowing person. But I'm finding this hard while racing around willy nilly, throwing on random drugstore make-up so I can look like a semblance of a human being. The good folks at *W3ll People* realize this is what happens in a busy world and they have a better way. Their products are all natural, all organic and don't use the nasty fillers and yucky preservatives that's in the stuff I've been slathering on. Not only do they have their own cosmetics, they also carry a wide range of other like-minded beauty products. This is what healthy thinking looks like.

covet:
w3ll people cosmetics:
   mineral creme foundation & concealer
   activist nourishing skin tonic
skin and hair care:
   ren
   arcona
   intelligent nutrients
escentric molecules perfumes

notes

notes

notes

notes

etc.

the eat.shop guides were created by kaie wellman and are published by cabazon books

eat.shop austin 3rd edition was written, researched and photographed by:
kaie wellman

editing: kevin de garmo   fact checking: alexandra sutinen
map and layout production: julia dickey and bryan wolf

kaie thx: marianne, joe and milo who make austin my favorite city in the whole world. thx also to elizabeth
and family and their pets, especially the enchanting mouse.

cabazon books: eat.shop austin 3rd edition
ISBN-13 9780984425310

every effort has been made to ensure the accuracy of the information in this book. however, certain details
are subject to change. please remember when using the guides that hours alter seasonally and sometimes
sadly, businesses close. the publisher cannot accept responsibility for any consequences arising from the
use of this book.

the *eat.shop guides* are distributed by independent publishers group in the u.s.: www.ipgbook.com
and in the united kingdom by portfolio books: www.portfoliobooks.com

to peer further into the world of *eat.shop* and to buy books, please visit: www.eatshopguides.com

PRINTED IN CHINA